THE PENGUIN POETS

SELVES

Philip Booth was born in 1925 in New Hampshire,
and grew up in that state and in Maine where he
now lives. He was educated at Dartmouth and
Columbia, taught at Wellesley, and for twenty-five
years was the senior poet in the Syracuse University
creative writing program. His books include *Letter
from a Distant Land, The Islanders, Weathers and
Edges, Margins, Available Light, Before Sleep,* and
Relations: Selected Poems 1950–1985. The recipient
of many honors, including two Guggenheim Fel-
lowships, an award from the National Institute of
Arts and Letters, and a Rockefeller Fellowship, in
1983 Philip Booth was elected a fellow of the Acad-
emy of American Poets.

· S E L V E S ·

· SELVES ·

new poems by

PHILIP BOOTH

PENGUIN BOOKS

PENGUIN BOOKS
Published by the Penguin Group
Viking Penguin, a division of Penguin Books USA Inc.,
375 Hudson Street, New York, New York 10014, U.S.A.
Penguin Books Ltd, 27 Wrights Lane, London W8 5TZ, England
Penguin Books Australia Ltd, Ringwood, Victoria, Australia
Penguin Books Canada Ltd, 2801 John Street,
Markham, Ontario, Canada L3R 1B4
Penguin Books (N.Z.) Ltd, 182–190 Wairau Road,
Auckland 10, New Zealand

Penguin Books Ltd, Registered Offices:
Harmondsworth, Middlesex, England

First published in the United States of America by
Viking Penguin, a division of Penguin Books USA Inc., 1990
Published in Penguin Books 1991

1   3   5   7   9   10   8   6   4   2

Page 75 constitutes an extension of this copyright page.

LIBRARY OF CONGRESS CATALOGING IN PUBLICATION DATA
Booth, Philip E.
Selves: new poems/by Philip Booth.
p.   cm.
ISBN 0 14 058.646 6
I. Title.
[PS3552.O647S45   1991]
811'.54—dc20   90–7683

Printed in the United States of America
Set in Garamond #3
Designed by Kathryn Parise

For
Kim Waller and Susan Ely
and
Jay Meek and Stephen Dunn

students, long ago,
by whom I'm still instructed

CONTENTS

IV

·SELVES·

What is terrible in life goes on somewhere
behind the scenes. . . . I am afraid to look at
the windows, for there is nothing that pains
me more than the spectacle of a happy family
sitting at table. . . .

Chekhov, *Gooseberries*

After-comers cannot guess the beauty been.
   Ten or twelve, only ten or twelve
      Strokes of havoc únselve
         The sweet especial scene. . . .

Hopkins, *Binsey Poplars*

And out of what one sees and hears and out
Of what one feels, who could have thought to make
So many selves. . . .

Stevens, *Esthétique du Mal*

REACHING IN

Reaching in to measure momentum,
the physicist alters the photon's position.

Reaching through midnight into the bathroom
my feet displace the shape of the dark.

My hand remembers a poem I gave you:
I made a poem I drew from the planet.

Reaching in, I trembled the landscape.
Where my words began is no longer home.

Weigh each word before you believe me.
However you read me you enter the story.

The rates at which our twined lives close
make waves in probability theory.

GARDEN

Went to a man in
his patch of garden.

Knew his brother was
in for surgery

over to the V.A.
Heard at the store

his sister, the
idiot one he'd

kept home forever,
died. Heard he

had to shoot his
dog the same day.

Told him I was
sorry, what

could I say. He
never spoke of the

sister; said when
he got up this

morning he saw
his dog couldn't,

said, *she was
parallel from*

the waist down.
His old eyes

wanted tears; mine
felt them come. Could

feel him feeling
how *Addie was*

parallel, up
in her head, from

when she was
born. He bent,

of a sudden,
folded himself

to grab some
old broccoli out

of his patch. And
stayed down, half-

kneeling. I tried
to stay, looking

around the garden
and, over the edge

of the world, out
at all the old sky.

WEDGE

No matter what edge
a woods man has given
his ax, time comes

when close to frozen
he has bigger chunks
to split, and switches

to maul and wedge,
the maul as thick as
the wedge at its

sharp end is thin.
Maul in hand, he
taps his wedge into

a check in the end-
grain, hauls back,
and swinging full-

arc, feels the blow
back to his shoulder
as steel strikes steel:

the tight grain gives
but refuses to
split. With his eye

on the wedge, as angry
as if wood knew to
reject it, he winds

his strength up again,
slightly off-balance.
Struck again, just off-

center, the wedge the
man can't do with-
out flips up into

the closing dark, and loses
itself, half out of sight
in this new year's first snow.

POOR

Back of the river,
feeding her stove,
every kitchen woman

knows how wood
dried two full seasons
gives, compared to green,

three times the heat.
And half the creosote.
Green cakes the pipe:

red-hot, the whole show
torches. Every husband
knows. But his saw or

his back or his truck
keeps giving out.
Or his woman's got

herself pregnant again,
or deer season's on, or
he had to fix his boat.

The night his house
went up like a rocket,
Moose Coombs, half-blinded,

said it: *A man like me
can't never afford
to get to be forehanded.*

FIGURING HOW

A tidal river.

Small planes all day, low
over islands, sliding across
spruce ridges.
            Took his canoe
after two beers, said he was going
clamming.
                    Divers in wetsuits,
standing around. The state cop
says the tide was all wrong,
nowhere near low enough to go
clamming.
                Where floodtide churns
at The Narrows, they found
his beat-up canoe, the paddles
nowhere.
            Today it's too roily
to see five feet. By now they figure
his body's snagged, or bouncing the bottom,
tumbled by tons of sea.
                        An old man,
been here before, says *in this cold*
it might be a week, might be a week
before he flies up.
                There's talk, too,
he already took off. Had it all figured:
left the kid with his mother, drank
with the boys, dumped his canoe.
                            By now
the boys say, by this third day,
he's maybe got to Saint John.
Or even Sacramento.

ZEROS

Three zeros coming up,
as the odometer turns
toward its new thousand.
Old movies, cars, pushing
2002, the number maybe
we'll get to, maybe we'll
not. As if numbers were
our destination, as if
we weren't close to lost.
As if it didn't matter
how we've already poisoned
the planet, invaded lovers,
born generations of micro-
chips, wired our lives to
suicide bombs, and still
told ourselves, year after
penultimate year, that there
will be survivors, that we'll
be the heroes who'll last.

PICKUP

Riding high.
                Over the blunt hood,
the headlights flat out. Gunrack
in the back window, radio scanning from
country to rock.
               I don't wanna let you
stop now.
          Joey, black CAT cap over
a thin spot, nestles his up, door to
door with the 4x4 Ram, in from
Nine Mile Corner.
              Do it, Baby, do it,
one more time.
          They talk options:
dual tube bumpers, lift kits,
Holley carbs. Maybe, after getting off
Friday, Daylite Off-Roaders. Or
fog lights.
           Bye, bye, Miss American Pie . . .
Joey punches the scan, and gets back
Wheeling.
          They talk low-end power,
desert radials, Hooker roll-bars,
the whole catalogue. Everything's far
except here: the glow of the panel,
the surge of the tach as they diddle,
idle, and then back off.
              There are girls
out there, from here to Iowa,
              waiting.

GAME

Between periods,
                    boys at the urinals,
boymen, menboys, telling AIDS jokes,
yelling *Ain't the game great.*
                              Jesus,
'djou see 'em rack that one up
right at the goal . . .
                    Freshman girls
in the stands,
                    screaming at referees
their fathers' utmost obscenities.
They must have learned
                    in the womb,
here or in Rome, at some earlier series,
limp but awake, the way,
                         in their parents' arms,
tonight's kids are fallen.
                         The other side
of the glass partition
                    the hurt players lie,
scattered like death at Antietam,
the trainers working over them, working
them over,
                    to get them back in the game.
O, its sheer violence,
                    our innate violence,
my anger squared in that tight arena
until I could not speak, or stay, but
walked myself out into winter sky,
                         out through
a door where a woman stamped me
with an ink pinetree,
                    sure,
since I'd paid so much,
I would come back in.

CIVILITIES

Kids in the city, where
there are only dogs, all
the time yelling it.
The same as country kids
yell, trying to be
tough; or women, proving
they have the same right
as men. Rich men pretending
they farm. None of them
within range of my grandmother,
whose proud Victorian bowels
never grumbled, who knew
right words, and which
to use when.
                    When Mr. Bowden
brought to her garden
cartloads of spring dressing,
it was presented, and
billed, as such. In her
presence, horse manure
was not a phrase he'd think
to use. Not that he didn't,
being from up in The County,
know deer droppings from
moosescat, or bearscat
from fox sign.
                    Fifty years gone,
this tilt backyard is still weighed
by their presence: Mr. Bowden
and Mrs. Hooke, bald pate
and ample bosom, their joined
civilities out inspecting
the edged border of her
perennial garden—the same
garden I'm just about to

turn over for turnips, beets,
and squash, being myself,
in the quick of spring,
already up to my boottops
in the back of the pickup,
forking out to my wife
lovely dark clods of cowdung.

LIGHTS

A bare winter, east of East Blue Hill,
as a man drives to work at first light:
the small houses set down like boulders

out in the blueberry barrens, the lights
just come on in small kitchens. The usual
raw dawn: firewood, coffee, smoke, no matter

what happened last night, what will happen
again. No shame more than the lack of it,
no room for love; the small houses

without outbuildings, no game shows on,
no soaps. Only the world, inside and out,
the hard news nobody wants to turn to.

Today or next week the father moving
his bowels, or the driver already awake,
will likely get let go at the mill.

Driving or driven, who can afford
to care? From house after house, the sun
still below the horizon, boys slow, girls early,

the kids start out toward the schoolbus stop.
As if to encourage some sun, the driver
headed to work flicks his headlights up.

UNITED STATES

All right, we are two nations.

Immaculate floors, ceilings broken
only by skylights. The insulated
walls, the soundless heat; and hidden
everywhere, a fan for every odor.

Of our two nations
that is one.
                    And you who will not
read this
                    presume you know the other.

OLD

Old, the old know cause to be bitter:

                they've seen

their children (as if they could tell)
insist they are growing deaf:

              they've found

old friends invent new friends
to prove the old don't matter:

            they have hardened

themselves to let memory rust out;
with only themselves to hold on to,

            they have grown

beyond any surprise;
to get their way

        they have aged again

to be children:
beyond control, they have gained

            control

of every last life save their own.
They know it can get no better.

FARVIEW HOME

For days she was calm, even on days
she wasn't sedated. But every few months,
on the full of the moon, or some said
the dark, she rampaged around in her wheelchair,
crying down corridors into the ceiling, *Why
God, why? O why God, why?*
                                        Then one day,
maybe two years ago, it was just before
Christmas, wheeling fast, her eyes straight ahead,
she put on the brake right outside my door
and, soft as her own dead mother, said *God,
up there, is there going to be two pianos.*

FALLBACK

An outdoor sign: under the big word FARVIEW
smaller letters spell *Intermediate Care.*

Year-round, now, she focuses at first light
on the sign, a wren of a woman looking out
from her cover. The night girl wakes her
at six for a washcloth, before
the day girls come on.
                    In the waking
they've shared for sixty-two years, she watches
Stanton getting his face washed, next to
the window in the same room. Out the window, over
the sign, rain thickens the lake, clouds
lie low on the mountain.
                    My body gone,
she thinks, *and his mind.*
                    When anyone visits,
his manners rise from the room's one armchair,
in his tweed suit, intact; she lies back
where she's been all day, her backbone so thin
the doctor jokes that X-rays can't find it.
She thinks her daughter may come today.
If she can. Labor Day she couldn't. Today
it's almost Hallowe'en, the Day Room filled
with paper pumpkins. Down at the nurse's station
the girls have carved a real one.
                    Out the window
not much color: the oaks dead bronze,
the marshgrass rusty. This morning she plans
how to set their watches tonight:
the old rule: *spring forward,*
            fall back.
            Now the night girl is back,
saying she's doing a double shift, covering
for Elsie.

        And the loons have been fewer, out
on the lake, and the Red Delicious are far
from what they were. Even at home,
the last year Elmer brought manure,
he said *Somethin's wrong with the bees,*
they're not comin round to spread pollen.
She watches Stanton wanting to talk to
the girl while she cranks up his bed;
watching, his curtain all the way back,
she can see his pale emeritus head risen into
the steel engraving of Harvard College.

                                        His mind,
she thinks, *and my body.*

                        Bringing trays now,
the night girl looks like a grebe. The woman
sips tea. Watching her husband try cereal,
she thinks back to summers they bird-watched,
Julys on Monhegan, a week once on Skye.

                                . . . out-of-
style beyond doubt, we were worn but fit.
His old Harris jacket, scratchy only in places.
She tries to smell the peat smell, the jacket he
laid out for picnics. But the night girl, bending
to take her tray, brings her home: the perfume
still lingering from whatever went on
before last night's shift.

                        And you at twenty,
who look away from us, wearing so cleverly little
(she smiles an idle small smile at her husband)
—how would you know we ever made love
in the sweetfern high on an island.

24

DEAR LIFE

The heart shivers to stay the mind's worry.
The mind skitters, not to look into itself.

The old doctor, wracked by his second stroke,
plumped-up in Room 112, not quite behind the screen,
his robe open, absently holding on to himself,
holding the way he held on as a three-year-old,
not knowing then what he cannot now speak:
how all of us, almost all, no matter how sorry,
still hold on for what used to be called dear life.

SHE

Attending the bed where he is near gone to ground,
consenting, in her high age, to every knowledge,
she pulls back the tides and recalls them.

She has kept the powers her whole life practiced:
an eye for cormorants rimming the outermost ledge,
waves she could read, and winds her whistle could call

to sail. She stories him what the cormorants told;
her voice spells a passage through days of fog,
her hand sounds a cove quick with stars. As his mind

closes to pain, he opens every eye to remember:
the white birds come to the island stillness, from space
beyond fog they have flown to her hand. He hears

against wind the distance she speaks from, yet all
that earth, between them, established: how she will wait,
consenting, until his own consent is accomplished.

CALLING

Across the bay, under its heavy Northwest sky,
horizon strips of deep light leaving the day.

The man on the shore stands in his own weather,
recalled by the light's low angle to the same sky,

the day years ago they scattered his father's ashes
across the Platte. He tries to figure how far today is

from the solstice. His watch shows two days to go,
and 4:06. *In another fifty-four minutes the rates*

will go down. He turns back home, sure beyond doubt:
I ought to call father. It's time I called father.

HEADING OUT

Beyond here there's no map.
How you get there is where
you'll arrive; how, dawn by
dawn, you can see your way
clear: in ponds, sky, just as
woods you walk through give
to fields. And rivers: beyond
all burning, you'll cross on bridges
you've long lugged with you.
Whatever your route, go lightly,
toward light. Once you give away
all save necessity, all's
mostly well: what you used to
believe you owned is nothing,
nothing beside how you've come
to feel. You've no need now
to give in or give out: the way
you're going your body seems
willing. Slowly as it may
otherwise tell you, whatever
it comes to you're bound to know.

RULE ONE

Rule One of all
rules one:
          No one ever knows
how much another hurts.
                 You.
Kate. Ray. Randall. Me.
                 The nurses
who were kind to you, the gaspump kid
across the bridge, the waitress here
this noon.
          No one ever knows.
Or maybe in a thousand, one
has the toughness to,
             to care,
to give beyond a selfish pity. Even
any given day,
            given weathers, detours,
chances of what look like luck,
if we feel bad
          we refuse the givens.
What blighted lives we lead.
              Or follow:
showering, feeding, changing shirts or
pants, working, as one used to say,
to make ourselves presentable.
                Partial
strangers to our painful selves,
we're still stranger to
diminished friends
when they appear
to hurt.
          How much we fail them,
failing to come close:
             a parent,
newly single, in Seattle;

an upstate poet in intensive care.
You. Blanche. Alvin. Sue.
                              Who hurts
and why.
                    Why we guess we know.
How much we never.

AMONG HOUSES

Among houses, none an adequate windbreak
for any other, a cold house
on a cold harbor, the Labrador current
icing its spilings on every tide.

Time seeps away. As nights gather,
the same argument over and over,
the last twenty years empty as Christmas.
Neither one what the other wants.

One day of sun and twelve of overcast,
the relentless nimbus of wanting change,
but the same wind picking at chinks,
the same small house grown smaller.

The emotions of shut-ins. They've insulated
to no avail: he will not let her be,
she will not let him feel. The old wind
catches its breath and starts in.

Christ, she thinks, *in my lifetime
has not risen. I continue to miss Him.*
He in his corner stiffens: *Who was I
before I went numb? Who did we used*

to be? They sleep separate dreams
and eat the same breakfast, same cold argument:
one day of argument, twelve of truce;
the same newspaper stuffed in chinks,

the same plastic tacked over the window.
Miles of drift-ice close in on the coast,
the world gone over the edge with sunset,
nothing to speak of left.

DARK

He knocked. He could hear her
come to the door.
Then, when it opened, there
was nobody there.

COUNTING THE WAYS

Beyond expectation, or toward,
three ways at least, other
than making love, to make love:

                              money

might count: the sheer freedom
to climax an evening with *Poire,*
after a Chablis *Grand Cru Vaudésir.*
And over and in between bottles,

                              mind:

not programmed intelligence, tuned
by degrees to Plato or Chekhov, but
mind-rise: turning through Brubeck to Mozart
and back, as the occasion offers: learning
the music as it is voiced, and gains
from the dark that surrounds;

                              laughter

not last or first, nor as a refusal
of tears, but risen from one's
inmost need to redeem: given
how dark invades, laughter of all
most surely:

                    before, during, and after.

DIRECTIONS

Imagine your insuranceman figuring how to say
the absence of imagination has to be imagined.
Now, without a vestige of laughter, presume to imagine
two people getting their bodies together: literally
scratching each other's back, touching this, feeling
for that, playing their tongues, their fingers, reaching
there or here, even using their toes, *and not laughing?*
Imagine not telling small lies into one ear or another;
or after due seasons, not smiling behind one's closed eyes.
Imagine, in fact, the comedy of a man making love to a woman,
making love over and over, for years, with a woman for whom
what's around the next corner, even on roads near home,
is repeatedly new, who joyfully forgets directions of
every kind; a woman for whom imagination is as simple
as Eden, as when, come early to bed, she sees a man in Augusta
sink a long putt on a black-and-white green on TV, and asks
of her husband, to his constant amazement, *Can you imagine?*

MARCH

Wet snow blinds the window,
blind gales pound the walls.
Feeling down stairs to

the woodstove, I feed my driest
hardwood to its blind fire.
And climb back up with thermals.

Blind nature storms my wakeful sleep
with what, to a man going
blind, comes close to light:

careless as she is, I can
feel her, and feel for her,
all this wild March night.

GLOVE

A good leather left one,
the one I've got left.
For two winters now I've warmed up
the car with one hand; every
November I look at my wife
and ask her straight out: *What
did you do with the right one?*
The whole first winter I kept on
waiting. This whole last winter
I half got used to the cold.
Now, in late March, good sun
keeps slacking the drifts: who cares
where the right one froze itself stiff
or went begging? Wherever it was
I let it get lost, it's gone,
gone for good. Just to keep
balances more or less even,
as of this morning
I threw out the left one.
Whatever it is I'm maybe
up to, next summer will tell.
I mean to get on as bare
as can be, as bare as
I've just become.

GIRL IN A GALLERY

She's looking away from me,
nearly in profile, smiling
at what I can't see;

her shoulder's tucked
forward, newly aware,
smiling, saying yes

to whatever it is.
Her forehead's highly
amused, her eyebrow happy.

One ear, perked through
her hair, singularly
ribboned, keeps up

a private laughter.
Her small breasts, tipped
to quick attention,

are at the moment
inclined to play:
neat waves near shore.

My presence she duly
disregards. Around
a considerable corner

from what delights her,
I only know how she
delights me: even as far

from her as I am,
my eyes return to
20/20, I can feel

my left thumb start
to laugh, my elbows
begin to cheer.

LONGINGS

To be young,
                both of you,
feeling it all begin,
beginning with somebody
newly close,
                the future
(as the song says)
entirely in your arms,
                            is nothing
beside feeling old, being
a man grown unsure,
and feeling next to
your body a girl embodying
it all at once,
                a girl
(as if she still were)
to whom your told life is
as new as her lips
are to you,
                O, there is nothing
so dear . . .
                unless it be
to live a while longer,
                and die
(as if for the first time)
                again
in the arms of the woman
with whom, against odds beyond
counting, you've dearly spent
some four thousand nights—or
twice as many, or half—
                and
in those nights come to learn

love over, learning, returning,
and turning over,

                    for the old rest
of your life.

WOMAN: A MIRROR

What do I do with the rest of my life?
What rest? No. My life's a textbook case,
as nobody need tell me. To save myself

I have to outlast all the fail-safe stuff
I padded marriage with, the common silliness
I thought was sense. I tried to rest my life

with how our daughters grew—while you, stiff
with ramrod pride, denied me equal promise.
I wanted you to tell me save myself,

but never knew what ways to ask. The gulf
we sailed was where I drowned (as if
you didn't know). The rest of this life

stills me; I'm bled dry, the skin that's left
is mirror to my own. As you, as
nobody need tell me. I brave myself

because I have due cause: all I face
I have to love for years, I have to ease,
admitting who I am to my own life.
Now nobody need tell me, save myself.

WATCHING OUT

As soon as whenever spring
begins, the marmalade cat
lugs home her next chipmunk.

As soon as snow's gone, she
brings him in: the same
dumb thing, over and over.

Another dumb chipmunk,
the same smart cat; from
wherever she finds him, she

parades him, homing straight
to the lawn. As soon as she
drops him, he thinks he's

got space to play with:
still half-stunned, he
starts back where he came from.

A quick paw, and he's back
with the cat. She keeps up
her game, plunk at

the lawn's dead center,
where any shelter's
equally far. Whenever

he runs, she swipes him back,
showing off to the house
her soft cat mouth.

She knows how we watch
out the picture window, she
knows the whole show's

going to get better.
It always does: drunk
with shock, the chipmunk

can't run five feet before
he squeaks back straight to
her eyelids; the dumb thing

thinks the cat is his mother.
Instead of running away
he runs to her. Over

and over, every spring:
the same big marmalade cat
putting on her spring show.

The same lawn, another
dumb chipmunk. And us,
watching out the same window.

ARGUMENT

Looked in on through the kitchen window—
who'd doubt that we were happy? Only
you and I, who know by what necessity

we argue. Given all I'm better at
than you, given all you are
I'm not, we equally contract to

argue. How else, as winter sunlight
cuts across our plates, do we
keep contact? Oh, in bed. But that

can't last forever. Not unless it, too,
becomes a variation on our single subject:
who brought the other down, down

to this gray leveling, this daily
burdening, and trading off, of guilt.
You want to argue even that; why not?

That neither one should ever win
is half the point. This and sex are all
we've learned entirely from each other.

SO

So, there's no way to be sure. Not
about much of anything. No more about
anyone else than ourselves. Perhaps
not even of death, except that it's bound
to happen. To you, yes; to me, us: the lot
of humankind, given how humankind sees it
from this near side. So what.

So nothing that we here and now
can perfectly know. Save, though the lens
our eyes raise, the old *here* and *now*.
The *this,* the *already-going* that moves us.
The red-shift we're constantly part of.
And why not? Between what we were, and
are going to be, is who and how we best love.

SIXTY

Spring hills, dark contraries:
a glade in a fall valley,
its one flower steeped with sun.

The there and here of her.
The soft where.
The sweet closeness when.

From dreams awake to turn to her.
Remembering, remembering.
And now again. Again.

·IV·

A POSTCARD FROM PORTSMOUTH

This still house:
                the gray sea light
tiding the window,
                  nobody's shade
yet up but mine;
                I read you in bed,
moved by your words
                to hear how
the harbormouth bell
                  constantly tolls
what we both know:
                  an inconstant music,
depths we can't sound,
                  lives
for which there is
                no safe passage,
the life we have left
                to keep
swimming out into.

SEEING

Ansel Adams postcards
from Maine to Kansas
and back

Far west of here
the dark foothills,
the high Sierra ridged
behind them. In a near field
a horse dark as hills,
grazing light.
                    I say
on my postcard *a glory*
of mountains, the mystery
of light absolute.
You say, by airmail
from halfway to there
from here, *I see*
what you mean.
                    You
who have been there:
the dark above pasture,
the snowfields above
the whole world; you
say you see and, after
love, sign your
simplest name.
                    Who
can I be to think to
scale mountains,
to think how mountains
lend scale to the hills,
and how both are lent scale
by the horse?
                    Who
can say how far

a man longs, after all
he is not, toward
all his want. I cannot
bear to. I only know,
far to the east, how
I know light and know
dark:
       whenever I
write you, you who've
never been here
where I am, I
see you, who cannot
know all you mean,
cantering that dark horse
across a small orchard,
the very small orchard
outside this back window.

WORDS MADE FROM LETTERS

Letters made of words, mailed letters
thickly definite.
                    But oh, to talk,
not to but with. Not stamps or phone,
but having made some harbor: say long after
dinner, and still longer; or walking
fields before:
                    along stone walls, a high field's
cold geometries in the small new snow.
Evenings, in each other's eyes, seeing
what gets said: the feel of words
we didn't know we knew to say, but found
we had, and did.
                    Odd words like *lie-lows,* or
say, *souvenirs,* as they come to mind from letters
written in a rainy light: like photographs,
not dark from absent knowledge, but caringly
made lucent: the way you tell how foxes greet
by *gekkering.*
                    Foxes met in your fields' Butterwort,
no doubt, or Bishop's Weed—on the hilly margin
where your eyelids ache to sleep, and
maybe dream a February story:
                    how wooden yawls,
cradled rail to rail in their great boatshed,
far up Center Harbor, all winter whisper to
each other how the summer went.
                    I hear you
as I read you, fingertip to fingertip against
the same gray page: the cadences of seasons,
your dogs' tails giving hearthroom to
the thump of your own heart.
                    I read you
soft and clear, even when, by card,
you write me from the Rockies to

reread *Job 38.* All that mountain power
and distance, yes. Rereading, I hear
Roethke's perfect theft of *Hath the rain*
a father?
              And back to you I offer:
Who hath put wisdom in the inward parts?
Or who hath given understanding to the heart?
God knows I cannot bind the Pleiades, nor
can you loose Orion's bands.
                                We make do with
old words and new:
                          Mesenteries, you write back
from weeks ago, you learned from your dead father
thirty falls before, drawing birds he'd shot,
asking, as you reached two fingers in,
                                        How come
the guts and giblets all come out a piece?
You say now he said
                          Mesenteries,
these pale visceral tissues which hold all in place,
which film these opalescent works so brightly coiled
in what you now recall as
                              death's own vegetable smell.
Well, we're bound to that,
                                in truth. But while
there's time I want to write I'm glad
to be alive in the same world as you,
                                        here where
there's, yes, a wisdom in the inward parts,
where something mesenteric loosely binds us,
where you, as words are bound to tell,
have given understanding to my heart.

MARCHES

Sun just up on the century's earliest equinox;
patchy snow in the woods, ice not yet out,
woodcock migrating into the alder thickets.
Far from woodsheds with less than a dry cord left,

the young winter-out on their counter-migrations:
wading the surf, getting wasted, pretending
they cannot die, and will not, as long as
their bodies tan, and burn to feel each other's.

Far in the desert, out to arrest their government,
twelve hundred women and men, hands linked against
a chainlink fence, give themselves to arrest.
Handcuffed, shunted to barbedwire camps, they delay

the test for twenty-four hours. In which new day
thousands of death-needles are passed, uncountable
lovers die shunned by their parents, hundreds of
children are born with systems in no way immune.

And millions of the rest of us, self-righteous
in the perfect democracy of backcountry roads, freeways,
and interstates, pass each other at life-span speeds;
or close, in opposing lanes, at a hundred-and-thirty,

trusting implicitly in simple self-interest, missing
each other, time after time, only by fragments of seconds,
as we move our lives, or dyings, another round toward
what March may be like in maybe the year 2000.

TIMES

No longer the old noon whistle,
the gold pocket watch, the Roman numerals
abroad on the kitchen clock. Those times

are over. Pressed now to whatever function,
the wrist's new chronograph, fraction-of-second
after fraction-of-second, flashes parts

of figures that transfigure as they move,
only to constantly tell what we better know,
how we ourselves are the measure of time:

time being the moment of waiting it takes
for the sun to go under the old horizon
it only just touched, the same distance

it took this morning, and the morning before,
to come wholly up from having first touched
the sky; as it will, we have to believe, the day

beyond this, each day barely different:
the field, and measure, of waiting as well
as arriving, even as stars arrive, through

and over the branches of our bare maple,
which will by sun become the same maple
changed green, when new stars turn over

and through and beyond, and then returned
from blank distance, come again into the tree
again bare, under which we, who thought only

to watch today's sun go under, find
our lives moved to discover how close
to arriving we must constantly wait.

THANKSGIVING

In the beginning was
with Mother,

                   swum into her sea,
perfect.

■

              After, not, save
when she let.

■

            Then lilac buds, fields
to wander, woods full of names she gave
to touch, to be touched by: hepatica
and bloodroot, dogtooth, trillium;
all April there to hold in eye, then
appleblossoms at floodtide,
                    the way a girl
and boy, embodied by each other.

■

Under trees, arrived to know, no more
to wonder what the wonder is. Held then,
letting wonder hold: the weather where
love happens, a room with all it houses.

■

A morning season, lasting weeks or seasons,
even years turned in to lives.
                  With family,
blood or no, the hard old gentleness,
the gentle wearing down. Or out.
As who'd not guess, within one's self,
endeared by loss to living how it goes.

■

The long becoming, then becoming gone.
How? Back into where?
                    Barely having grown
toward love: hating
                    to lose any measure.
How leave? How stay
                    what's left? No way
save the old ways,
                    always: not giving in
but to, and being so returned.

                    ■

                    And turned,
too, into memory, becoming
finally gray withal. Yet gentle, gentled,
feeling one's self felt in generations
barely born,
                    the way a blind pianist
feels dark music, joyful as he jazzes
how it feels: how all, befallen
finally, rise within us,
                    woken in us,
nightly, when we let them come.

                    ■

                    Father,
here at heart, where I have you, you
beyond all want but yearning inward to
be part, again to be embodied:
                    as in
a grandson's eyes,
                    as you through me here are,
given this Thanksgiving:
                    this yearly day,
                    this table where

a daughter's husband, asked to ask the blessing,
gathers hands beside him to complete the ring,
quotes Emily here in Amherst and invites us all,
blessed by tears and laughter, to share with her
   . . . *a sunny mind,*
Thy windy will to bear.

     ■

       Here where we
bear each other, in us each
the heart beats its small code:
       so far

so good, so far so
good, so far . . .
    for now, for
now, we give up tears
and, being gathered, sing.

PROVISIONS

The paperback somebody left on the plane
tells what you'll need to carry on your person:
immune seeds in a shielded packet, something of value
to barter, a hardener to refill your own teeth.
The book suggests what weapon to take against
your own kind. And the canteen of water from
pipes still safe; salve for your skin;
a drug, at any cost, against immediate pain.
You already know you won't want for matches;
you will have thought, long since, of boots
with impervious soles, fit for the distance;
repellent clothes, a balaclava, or thick-brimmed
hat, toward whatever the season may be.
Proud flesh will be your least of crises,
but take curved scissors for what you'll need
to debride. And, yes, dried food, for twice as long
as you think. The book says *Go, leave objects behind.*
That much is true. Leave the book first of all;
it forgets to say what you cannot forget: that there's
no place to go. Whether or not you go or stay, make
an eyeshield, pocket next to your heart whatever
poems you might now think to copy, keep with you
what's left of Thoreau. And since no one
but Bach can hold in mind all the Bach
one is bound to need, you might well practice
carrying his simplest tune: the small dance in G
that Anna Magdalena every morning sang
to ease her firstborn son. Carry that music, always,
in your head. What memory you have is all you'll have left;
in whatever mornings there are, you'll have for as long
as you possibly can simply to hum to yourself.

WANTING

Coastal rain, an iron sky.
Granite mainland, granite island.
It's too cold, I'm too cold,

to row across to the mainland.
The pickup needs an inspection;
I ought to row over across and

drive her to Gray for a sticker.
Let it wait. There's still time.
There's time this morning to

read the whole day, to read
the cold rain, the old sky, the who-
do-I-think-I-am. Between five

and seven, the crown of the day
no matter what weather, who can afford
less wonder? Or bear any more?

I'm in the kitchen, belonging
with what doesn't know me, so far
as I know: pots and pans that

heat up and cool, belonging by how
I feel about them, not how they
maybe feel about me. Beings who

differently breathe, we humans
contract—in and out—to expand
all our lives. Who in hell would I be

if I couldn't imagine, imagine
the range of this moment in
the spun flight, the spun life

of the planet? It's here, when
anyone pays due attention:
here now, there then in the now

where anyone opens to feel it.
Now, shaving, I long to pay back
what I owe, however much, in

the mirror, I find myself
wanting. Wanting in all
directions, across distance

measured in minutes as well
as degrees. Now, out doors,
out under ospreys wheeling over

a tide stream, searching the shallows
for alewives, I look up with
my own hunger. *Hunger:* how

can I mean it, given
lives starving? I want to mean
how-can-I-not, to have

their lives at heart, stretching
not reaching as their lives
contract, while my life

is weighed with alternatives.
How can I possibly mean,
give what to whom, given

this glassy sea I cannot
see much beyond, this island
that embraces my waking: this spruce,

deermoss, this lichen, and you
in time I want far from here
to touch, the you in far different light

who is differently focused, more
or less caring or careless, while
I move under the high pitched birds

and—by long inclination—lift
myself over a dark march of ants
crossing the bedrock granite.

SHORT DAY

The calm deck of a cradled
boat. Sea-smoke out over

the harbor, giving way
to the full-flood sun.

Been between the machine-
shop and boat since seven,

wanting what nut will
fit an enginemount stud

I can feel but not see.
½ was too small, ⁹⁄₁₆ths

too big, so I came up
out into sky and went

for metric. The blue
and thin cirrus high

beyond measure. The boat-
yard mallards glad to

be tame now that duck
season's on. Guns firing

like war out in the
islands. Found metric

hex nuts in the gray
drawer where wrench sets

belong. And a thread-
gauge from Sears.

Took a 12 and 14,
fine thread and coarse,

clean as the whistle
of two pairs of loons,

fishing out in the channel.
Hard to figure how they

stay paired. But they
do. The stainless nuts

warm in infinite
sunlight, my head

warms to morning;
I climb back topside

and dive again into
the dark, my hand

fishing aft to feel
the rear mount. The 12's

too snug, the 14 floats
like the 9/16ths. She

has to be a 13. Which,
once I feel the thread

with the gauge, if
I can, will take me

all the rest of
the morning to go

to pick up in Green
Harbor. One #13

stainless hex nut.
Focused on this

tame purpose, I
come up bright as

a loon, floating where
ever the rest of me

wants: part of me here,
part beyond any labor

or dark, flown beyond
loons or mallards or

islands, to distances
beyond gauging, save

as I have them
at heart. I give

myself leave to
be out there, far

offshore where,
over the labyrin-

thine waves, a seabird
without a name

circles, her wings quieting
to calm the sea

as she comes in
to light.

TWO

Out of doors. Climbed out
of towns. Toward sea.

Or rivering. Toward waves
of grass. Near trees.

Being. Being so exposed.
The gravity of two

becoming stormed. Two.
The power of it: powers

raised by powers. Rain
not yet come, sleet

not yet come, the sun
both gone and born.

The planet tilted back
to gather heat. Arms

clasping sky to body,
length by length, light

to light: the air
transformed, the field

transformed: bared now,
the sky let go, stunned

by their own beauty
on the island where

love happens, two
let springtides quicken,

flood, and come to
an unutterable calm—

Who can say
what to each other

other lovers say
before they sleep?

Or waking, still
believe? One

only half knows
how two feel—

for that new fraction of
their lives before,

fulfilled, the earth
again returns to world.

SEA LEVEL

Late May. Morning fog after
good stars, the village shoreline
long at springtide, still ebbing.

Between the beachstones, years
of china, green bits of pre-
returnable bottles, rusted rebar,

and scallop shells shucked over-
board from last winter's catch.
On every ebb, it's no and every

season: generations of barnacles,
periwinkles clinging to brickyard shards
churned downriver from a gone century.

The sun's coming, coming fast.
I'm on my slow way to work, my eye
on harbor seals hauled out on

the middleground ledge. Three seals,
maybe four; three and a pup or
three and a sea-shaped rock.

Hard to tell at this angle, given
the sea level glare. If it weren't
for the fallen coal wharf's old spilings,

a long-legged fence between me
and the seals, I might walk out
among them, pull down the fogged sun

for my halo, and—when the tide came—
simply keep walking across.
But I'm here, who I am, given

this day: as the fog burns off
top first, I can hear, close in,
the snuffle and low yelp of seals;

and from the far shore, a mile through
haze now blindingly bright, men's voices,
as clear as if I might know them,

sound across to me, sound down into
my woken life, today irreversibly
flooding, incomparable in its own light.

PRESENCE

after George Oppen

That we are here: that we can question who
we are, where; that we relate to how deer

once small have grown bold in our back garden;
that we can ask, ask even ourselves, how

to the other we may appear, here in the always near place
we seem to ourselves to inhabit, who sleep toward

and wake from steeped hills, the sea opening into our eyes
the infinite possibility of infinity

we believe we're neither beyond nor shy of,
here as we are, without doubt, amid then, there,

and now, falling through dark into light, and back,
against which we cannot defend, wish as we might, as we do.

Still, as the physicist said, *the mystery is*
that we are here, here at all, still bearing with,

and borne by, all we try to make sense of:
this evening two does and a fawn who browse

the head lettuce we once thought was ours.
But no. As we chase them off mildly, and make

an odd salad of what they left us, the old stars
come casually out, and we see near and far we own nothing:

it's us who belong to all else; who, given this day,
are touched by, and touch, our tenderest knowing,

our lives incalculably dear as we feel for each other,
our skin no more or less thin than that of redwing,

rainbow, star-nose, or whitethroat, enfolded like us
in the valleys and waves of this irrefutable planet.

ACKNOWLEDGMENTS

For permission to reprint these poems, some in versions now slightly revised, thanks to editors of the journals in which they first appeared:

"United States," *America*; "Pickup," "Wedge," "Short Day," "Marches," "March," "Calling," "Dear Life," "Farview Home," "Fallback," "Provisions," "Sea Level," "Zeros," *The American Poetry Review*; "Argument," *Antaeus*; "Sixty," *The Atlantic*; "Watching Out," *Blueline*; "Reaching In," *Denver Quarterly*; "Woman: a Mirror," "Seeing," "Words Made from Letters," *The Georgia Review*; "Poor," "Civilities," "Lights," *The Harvard Magazine*; "Game," *Ironwood*; "Thanksgiving," *The New England Review/Bread Loaf Quarterly*; "Counting the Ways," *The New Republic*; "Garden," *North Dakota Quarterly*; "So," *Pequod*; "Figuring How," "Wanting," *Ploughshares*; "Presence," "Rule One," "Glove," "Heading Out," "Times," *Poetry*; "She," "A Postcard from Portsmouth," "Directions," "Girl in a Gallery," "Longings," *Poetry Northwest*; "Old," *The Seattle Review*; "Among Houses," *Tendril*.

For permission to use in "Pickup" a line from "American Pie" by Don McLean, thanks to him and to his publishers, Mayday Music/Benny Bird Co., Inc. The epigraph from "Esthétique du Mal" is from *The Collected Poems of Wallace Stevens*, copyright 1954 by Wallace Stevens, and is reprinted by kind permission of Alfred A. Knopf, Inc. I want also to note that the second line of "Directions" is a distortion of a line by Wallace Stevens; that the first four words of "Presence" reverse the percept which informs the third line of George Oppen's "Psalm"; and that my "Counting the Ways" is for Ward Just and Virginia, the woman in his novella "Cease Fire" from whom the first three lines of this poem derive.

Thanks to Margaret Booth for astute first readings; and to Patricia Fowler for critically acute rereadings. And to Stephen Dunn, Susan Ely, Jay Meek, and Kim Waller thanks for how they have read, listened, heard, and returned me their own words for close to thirty years.

FOR THE BEST IN PAPERBACKS, LOOK FOR THE 🐧

In every corner of the world, on every subject under the sun, Penguin represents quality and variety—the very best in publishing today.

For complete information about books available from Penguin—including Pelicans, Puffins, Peregrines, and Penguin Classics—and how to order them, write to us at the appropriate address below. Please note that for copyright reasons the selection of books varies from country to country.

In the United Kingdom: For a complete list of books available from Penguin in the U.K., please write to *Dept E.P., Penguin Books Ltd, Harmondsworth, Middlesex, UB7 0DA*.

In the United States: For a complete list of books available from Penguin in the U.S., please write to *Dept BA, Penguin*, Box 120, Bergenfield, New Jersey 07621-0120.

In Canada: For a complete list of books available from Penguin in Canada, please write to *Penguin Books Ltd, 2801 John Street, Markham, Ontario L3R 1B4*.

In Australia: For a complete list of books available from Penguin in Australia, please write to the *Marketing Department, Penguin Books Ltd, P.O. Box 257, Ringwood, Victoria 3134*.

In New Zealand: For a complete list of books available from Penguin in New Zealand, please write to the *Marketing Department, Penguin Books (NZ) Ltd, Private Bag, Takapuna, Auckland 9*.

In India: For a complete list of books available from Penguin, please write to *Penguin Overseas Ltd, 706 Eros Apartments, 56 Nehru Place, New Delhi, 110019*.

In Holland: For a complete list of books available from Penguin in Holland, please write to *Penguin Books Nederland B.V., Postbus 195, NL-1380AD Weesp, Netherlands*.

In Germany: For a complete list of books available from Penguin, please write to *Penguin Books Ltd, Friedrichstrasse 10-12, D-6000 Frankfurt Main 1, Federal Republic of Germany*.

In Spain: For a complete list of books available from Penguin in Spain, please write to *Longman, Penguin España, Calle San Nicolas 15, E-28013 Madrid, Spain*.

In Japan: For a complete list of books available from Penguin in Japan, please write to *Longman Penguin Japan Co Ltd, Yamaguchi Building, 2-12-9 Kanda Jimbocho, Chiyoda-Ku, Tokyo 101, Japan*.

FOR THE BEST POETRY, LOOK FOR THE ⊕

FOR THE BEST POETRY, LOOK FOR THE 🐧

☐ **TANGO**
Daniel Halpern

The poems in Daniel Halpern's sixth collection explore encounters with land-scape, with friendship, with isolation, and with love and death.

"*Tango* has its own definite character and imprint—real, original, and strong."
— Robert Penn Warren

88 pages *ISBN: 0-14-058588-5* **$10.95**

☐ **LAST WALTZ IN SANTIAGO**
And Other Poems of Exile and Disappearance
Ariel Dorfman

From the land of Pablo Neruda, here is a searing collection of poems about torture and resistance, horror and hope. In Ariel Dorfman's world, men and women choose between leaving their country or dying for it.

"Deeply moving . . . stark and at the same time oddly radiant"
— Margaret Atwood *78 pages* *ISBN: 0-14-058608-3* **$8.95**

☐ **CEMETERY NIGHTS**
Stephen Dobyns

In his sixth book of poems, Stephen Dobyns explores a full range of human experience—from fabulous storytelling to explosive passions of domestic life, from vital distortions of familiar myths to strange tableaux of creation and death.

"Dobyns has fashioned his remarkable poems into a real book, not simply a collection." — *The New York Times Book Review*
100 pages *ISBN: 0-14-058584-2* **$9.95**

☐ **AGAINST ROMANCE**
Michael Blumenthal

A new collection from the winner of the Academy of American Poets Peter I.B. Lavan Younger Poets Award, *Against Romance* explores the possibilities for love in an unromantic time and an indifferent, beautiful universe.

"Advancing by leaps and loopholes of inference, Michael Blumenthal's poems . . . are never far from joy." — Anthony Hecht
108 pages *ISBN: 0-14-058600-8* **$8.95**